CupOfTherapy™

Self-Care
Every Day

First published in Great Britain in 2022 by
Greenfinch
An imprint of Quercus Editions Ltd
Carmelite House
50 Victoria Embankment
London EC4Y 0DZ

An Hachette UK company

The moral right of Antti Ervasti and Matti Pikkujämsä to be identified as the authors of this work has been asserted in accordance with the Copyright, Designs and Patents Act, 1988.

A CIP catalogue record for this book is available from the British Library

HB ISBN 978-1-52941-731-9
eBook ISBN 978-1-52941-732-6

10 9 8 7 6 5 4 3 2 1

Typeset in Minion Pro by Ginny Zeal

Printed and bound in China by C&C Offset Printing Co., Ltd.

Papers used by Greenfinch are from well-managed forests and other responsible sources.

CupOfTherapy™

Self-Care Every Day

Daily doses of kindness and self-compassion

Antti Ervasti and Matti Pikkujämsä

greenfinch

'The sweet, not totally perfect and expressive animal figures adventuring in the CupOfTherapy illustrations provide us with an easy opportunity to relate various happy, embarrassing and even painful situations we face in everyday life. We often tend to hide difficult life situations and mental health problems. Warmth and humour are often the best antidotes when trying to silence the inner critic. It may help us recognise and accept our own vulnerability when we see heart-warming animal figures resembling our current life situation.'

Helena Aatsinki
Occupational Health Doctor,
Sleep Medicine Specialist,
Psychotherapist, Clinical Supervisor

Contents

Morning

Life and feelings
hour by hour.

Time flies by and life goes on minute by minute, second by second no matter whether we are in a meeting or lying on the sofa at home. We change, the world changes, our work changes, our relationships change. Connections and the bonds we share with our closest ones bring us balance when time gets away from us. A message from a loved one may come at a crucial point in time and serve as a source of strength, more precious than we could have guessed. Being aware of going through this life together brings us feelings of safety and stability.

Mental health and sleep go hand in hand, because day-to-day challenges are always easier to face when well-rested. Quality sleep is also crucial for physical well-being. Everyday problems can easily translate into sleep problems: stress and pressure interrupt sleep, and instead of a gentle start to our day, we wake up in the middle of the night or find ourselves exhausted in the morning due to poor-quality rest. A well-rested mind can solve everyday problems better than a tired one, so pay attention to the quality and quantity of sleep and rest you are getting.

We are fragile little beings as we wake up to a new morning. The dream world of the night has not completely receded, while the challenges of the day already begin to avalanche into your mind. Be kind to yourself and create your own morning self-care routine. Your body may need a gentle stretch and your mind a quiet exercise in gratitude. For some, just watching their porridge simmer on the stove is like meditation, while others prefer a quiet moment with the morning newspaper. Pamper and nurture your delicate morning self in the ways that suit you best.

Be kind to yourself every morning.

'You are ugly. You are lazy. There are no beautiful clothes in your closet. You do not know how to do anything.' Imagine hearing someone else talk to you like this in the morning – how would it make you feel? Yet so many people speak to themselves this way. Our inner voice is often harsh. Think about whether you want to accept this discouraging and blunt tone, or if you could be reassuring and kind to yourself. It is much more constructive to focus on your strengths and cultivate those; you can also discover new good things about yourself when you seek the positive. You can do whatever you set your mind to.

Sometimes you need support, and sometimes you will be the one to support others. Compassion, words of encouragement, and small actions can make a huge difference to your co-worker, partner or friend. Awareness that we are not alone through such actions empowers us and creates hope for the better. Your presence is important.

Good morning my sunshine.

When we constantly spend time in each other's company, disagreements and unkind words can arise. None of us are perfect in our communication, but luckily it is always possible to defuse conflict to prevent it escalating. The most important thing is to notice when you need to say 'sorry' so the other person does not have to wait for an apology.

The evil
eye is
staring
at me.

Whose voice, whose gaze do you obey? We are often our own worst critics. The voice inside may say, 'There is no way you will succeed, don't flatter yourself.' Continuous self-monitoring can go into overdrive and destroy self-esteem and self-confidence. Think about whether the voice of your inner critic is truly your own, or maybe someone else's that you have adopted. Try to set aside the harsh self-critic for a moment and focus on building self-esteem instead. It may be difficult to unlearn the habit, but it is important to try. Shift your focus from yourself to your surroundings and others around you. Make self-compassion a virtue. Change your inner voice to one of support that says, 'You've got this, I believe in you!'

positivity
on
repeat.

Positive thinking creates more positivity. At times, it feels that as humans we are programmed to focus on worries and threats, and it takes extreme effort to see the up side. But if we work together to create a circle of positivity and focus on the things that are good, we will be better off even in the midst of adversity. Positive, creative thinking thrives when built on the steady foundation of nourishing everyday routines.

My own morning
pyjama party.

Music, dance and movement are known to be good for the body as well as the mind. You can allow yourself to go wild in the privacy of your own home, so why not do your morning routine accompanied by your favourite music? Dance if you feel like it! Upbeat melodies and rhythms have a beneficial impact on our thought process, and movement gently wakes up the body after a good night's sleep. With music, you can steer your emotions and consciously generate positive thinking.

Start the day
with
sunny
thoughts.

Do you find yourself regularly feeling down in the morning? Could this emotion be caused by some deeper concerns? Some of us are more prone to worry than others, creating a cycle where we worry nonstop and can no longer see any reason to be grateful. As if something bad would happen if we did not worry constantly! It is important to pause and think about this. If worrying is taking up too much of your resources, break this negative cycle by finding small ways to maintain a positive sense of control over your everyday life – write a to-do list or chose a small achievable task to kick-start your day. Think of ways you can find hope and curiosity in your daily life, and focus on these positives as you start your day.

Chaotic, stressful mornings may be a cliché, but for many of us, they are also a reality. We often leave things to the last minute, as if trying to tempt fate! Remember, looking ahead and planning is not only a matter of self-care, but also a little everyday luxury – allowing yourself even just 10 minutes of extra time in your morning routine brings a sense of unhurriedness that soothes and prepares the mind for the new day. Find ways to ease your morning tasks, such as choosing your clothes or setting the breakfast table the evening before.

It's only
a Monday
morning.

Weekends are often very social, and we do not have to worry about time as much as during the working week. It can feel difficult returning to the weekday rhythm after a weekend or holiday, and we may suffer from social jetlag. The pressures of working life are reflected in the increased importance of leisure time. To counter the Monday blues, try to use your work and everyday life as a safe foundation that you can build your family life and relationships on. Take a new attitude toward work, too: being away from the others for a while is healthy, and having something to look forward to cheers you up! There will always be another weekend.

Let's not forget what is the most important.

In a relationship, everyday life is where connection and intimacy are created. How we connect – or not – in the morning leaves an emotional trace throughout the day, which influences how present we are at work. In the mornings, be caring and considerate towards your partner; the fresh memory of a goodbye kiss or a morning hug can act as fuel for the day. Morning quarrels over insignificant little things can linger and snowball into putting your foot in your mouth at the workplace as well.

There are so many reasons to be thankful.

Happiness is made up of the little everyday moments, but it is difficult to be delighted by something that is present all the time. Many of us are only aware of our happiness once it is at risk. The possibility of losing work, dealing with an illness or other setbacks make ordinary everyday life seem like a great celebration. There may come a time when you miss those completely ordinary weekdays that have passed. Recognizing those everyday joys even when everything is going well helps to foster a greater sense of well-being. Could everyday life smoothly moving forward give you reason enough to be happy and grateful?

Unemployment, be it short-term or long-term, requires preserving our feelings of self-worth and confidence for the future. Even if you do not have regular working hours, it is good to find a daily routine that suits you. For example, waking up at a certain time or exercising regularly can help provide structure to your day. It is possible to use the free time to your advantage and perhaps to rethink your career. Sometimes a crisis offers new opportunities – maintaining a positive outlook and believing in those opportunities are key. You should not let the employment situation make you bitter, neither should you blame yourself. In these circumstances, it is possible to re-evaluate your life and even retrain for something new.

The Selection of Morning passions

Jazz

Diary

Poems

Knitting

Mornings influence how our day is going to play out. No matter if your commute takes fifteen minutes or an hour and a half, dedicate this time for the well-being of your mind. Do you love poetry? Does knitting give you peace of mind? How would your favourite song sound in the morning traffic of a grey weekday morning? Do not limit your passions to the evenings – make them a part of your morning routine. Peaceful mornings create mental space for the demanding challenges of the day, while stressful mornings splinter your concentration even before the day has really started.

True hope needs action.

Living according to your values helps to unlock the full potential of your mind. It manifests as creativity and positive energy at work as well as in other areas of life. Actions do not have to be grand to be meaningful: if you want to combat climate change, bike to work, choose a vegetarian option at lunch and print fewer pages. All of these choices are concrete everyday actions that are good for our planet.

Enjoy the morning air.

You learn to see beauty first by looking for it. When was the last time you admired the colours of the sunrise? Is there a tree on your commute that over the course of the year shoots leaves, bursts into bloom and then shines in all its autumn colours? Children have a phenomenal ability to see fascinating details in their surroundings, and us adults would do well to take our eyes off our phones sometimes to pay attention to what is around us. Make an intentional decision to be present in a time and place. Take note of your daily environment and enjoy the beauty of it.

Protect your optimism by prioritizing positive action, and do not make any room for laziness or cynicism. By consistently following your conscience, it makes it easier to do the right thing, even if the action seems naive or trivial. Positive action can mean anything from buying coffee in your own cup instead of using disposable cups to starting a recycling scheme at work. Ultimately, small everyday actions are part of a larger whole and a way to start believing in your ability to make a change.

We do not all move at the same pace, and there should be room for individual differences in our efficiency-oriented working life. For example, constantly arriving late to work should not be ignored, but being sensitive to the situation it is worth looking at the bigger picture and taking the employee's personal circumstances into account. With an open and welcoming atmosphere in the workplace, it is safe to talk about challenges and weaknesses and to work together to find meaningful solutions.

Not all of us are at our best in the morning, and we all take different amounts of time to get into the day. Even if your colleague's bubbly morning energy seems annoying, give them room, because your prime time will be later. Perhaps you get your most creative ideas later in the day? Do not get discouraged by the excited early riser, just allow yourself to take a role as a listener. Different personalities enrich workplaces and communities and should be given the space to do so.

At work

The first day at a new workplace comes with a lot of expectations. It is perfectly natural to feel nervous about something new! Give yourself time to adjust to your new job and work community, and remember that you have been chosen for your job because you have a lot to give. Try not be overwhelmed or jump to hasty conclusions based on one day, and do not be too harsh on yourself. Most importantly, enjoy the new opportunities and get excited!

All
parts
are
needed.

The workplace is like a body, all parts of which are vital for the smooth running of the whole. Likewise, everyone's skills are important for a workplace to succeed. Visible and invisible actions are equally as important. Be sure to acknowledge – aloud – the value of seemingly small inputs, because without small actions, great things cannot be achieved.

Our differences are our strengths.

Different personalities are needed in the workplace. Certain tasks favour certain personality types; therefore, people who have different modes of expressing themselves can find a way to work together, as long as everyone is open and involved. In order to reach the best end result, a talented manager knows how to form teams in which everyone can shine and be themselves. Diversity, not just profit responsibility, enriches a workplace too.

Our home, our responsibility.

More and more workplaces are operating globally and taking responsibility for the future of the planet. One of the most pressing concerns today is the effect our individual actions have on the larger whole. The workplace is no different. Companies create their culture through their ethical choices. Does a company support the values of its employees, or does it only aim to maximize profits? The more a community shares the same values, the better the results – and the stronger the community.

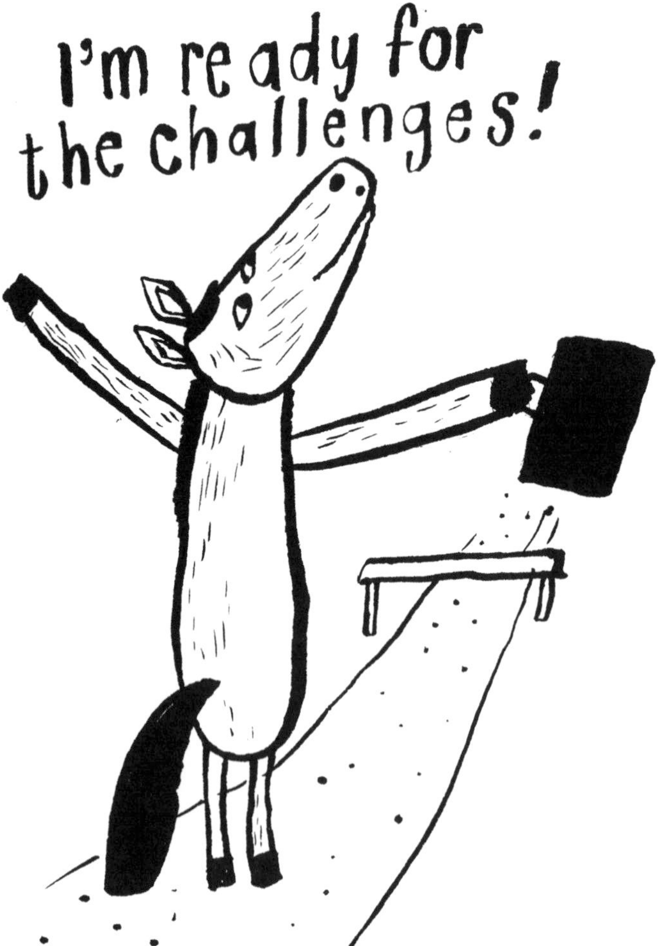
I'm ready for
the challenges!

Life should not be merely about going through the motions. Very few people are happy to go to work if it only feels like monotonously repeating the same tasks. We need a certain number of obstacles to overcome and goals to achieve. A positive, motivated employee is ready for new challenges. We all need to experience success and feel trusted by others to make good decisions.

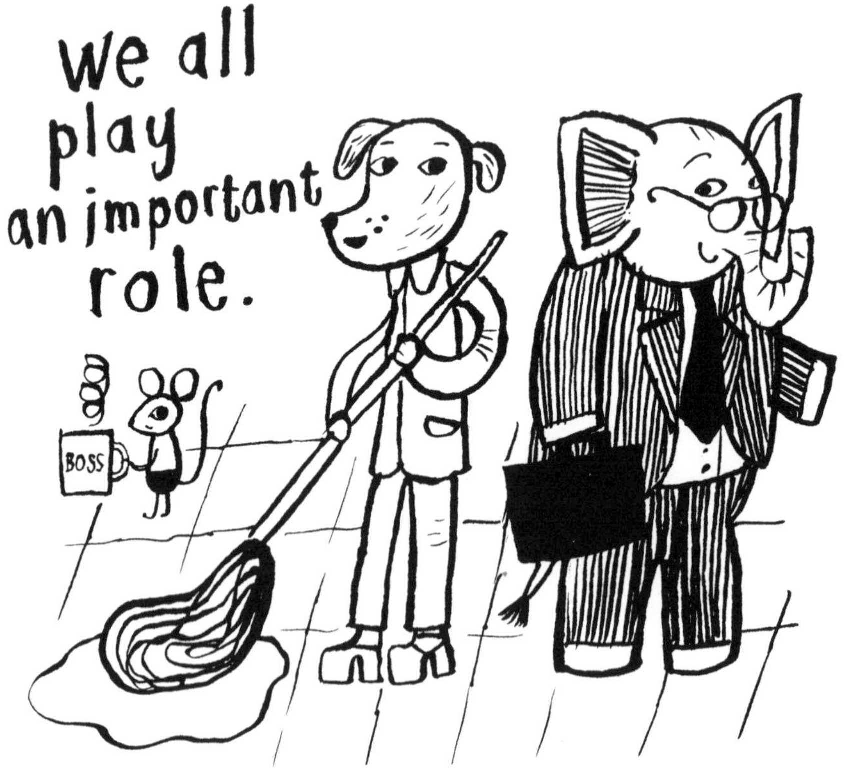
we all
play
an important
role.
BOSS

Words like 'boss' and 'employee' can have a negative impact when defining our positions. None of us are above or below others. Our job descriptions are very different, and we should all do our work with respect for ourselves and for others. Professional pride is ultimately not about position or pay, but about values, and the true meaning of things cannot be measured by external attributes or titles. Each of us has our own important role and we all deserve full respect for it.

A skillful leader also has good emotional skills. They understand their position as one part of a team comprised of various personalities with different needs and circumstances. A good leader does not live in an ivory tower, but values even the smallest contribution from each and every team member. It is easy to hide behind a higher-status position and avoid responsibility by blaming others, but creating a good work environment happens through genuine appreciation, trust and listening. Humility is a great strength.

The canvas is ready, time to create a masterpiece.

A well-known fact amongst artists is that standing around waiting for inspiration to strike does not help – the best way to find inspiration is through working. You can trick yourself into getting a job done by breaking the task into smaller pieces. Before you start, clean up your desk and make your working conditions as comfortable as possible. Then, when you start working, your mind will be like a blank canvas, and no blank canvas is worth being afraid of – trust the great power of the mind and your abilities!

Too rarely do we give recognition to ourselves. We only focus on moving forward, even though pausing and acknowledging at our achievements with pride is an essential part of maintaining motivation. Completing a project is always worth a celebration! We do better with future endeavours, too, if we have experienced finishing a project or task as a true success and a rewarding experience. Saying 'thank you' to yourself is the perfect way to do this.

There are loud and quiet personalities within a workplace. Friendly voices, and some that are more critical. It is frustrating if you notice that your voice is not being heard and your words seem powerless. Take the courageous step of speaking up – even just by saying the right, perhaps daring, but thoughtful word. It can be a simple 'no'. Listen to and follow the voice of your conscience and set the boundary where it feels right.

Envy, the feeling we are often too embarrassed to talk about, wants to tell you something. Listen to it. Treat it with compassion and analyse its message calmly and constructively. Do you feel that your potential is poorly understood, or that you have not truly been seen? Have you lost your sense of purpose? You must not give envy the power to control your feelings and behaviour, instead use it as a tool to identify if there are areas in your life that may benefit from more attention or a change. Practice being happy for others, it is a skill that is easily overlooked.

If you find yourself seething with anger when you see your colleague succeed, pause and consider that their accomplishments will drive you forward as well. Think of the irritation as a mirror and redirect your gaze at yourself; what kind of person do you see when you are irritated? Do you detect feelings of inadequacy or uncertainty about the future? Remember that while some build their careers with big steps, there is also important, significant work done at the grassroots level. Everyone chooses their own way to be noticed. Are you working on creating the right content or just focusing on the attention?

Comparison and competition are inevitable in working life. Sometimes even close colleagues find themselves in an awkward situation where they are ranked in some way. The situation may seem devastating, causing feelings of self-deprecation or uncertainty. How do you maintain your confidence under pressure? New challenges, such as a job search process, are an opportunity to grow mentally and professionally, and to gain new experience and confidence in our skills. Ask yourself, 'Why would I not pursue this job that I fulfil the criteria and would be a good fit for?'

In order to get work done effectively you need to be fully present. This leads to better motivation and ultimately success, as it is also a prerequisite for achieveing a productive flow state. When we enter into a contract of employment, we promise to give our time as well as our presence. This does not mean spending hours on social media during the workday. Save it for your free time, so you feel like you have truly earned it – time off feels especially well-deserved when all the work is done!

Few workplaces adequately address the issue of how much an employee should be available. Expectations of logging on are often left to the employee's own interpretation, and some may overdo being online just in case. This can lead to burnout and is an unproductive way of working. Replying to an email as soon as we receive it, does not make us any more conscientious or better employees than those who respond later in the day. It is important to focus on the task at hand and to be able to be offline without guilt.

Knowing how to take critical feedback is part of being a professional. Often, we learn through our mistakes – we did our best, but the feedback tells a different story. Criticism may undermine your belief in your abilities momentarily, but remember that criticism falls on everyone sometimes. It is not you as a person who is criticized, but your work. When you know how to receive critical feedback, you can use it as a chance to grow your expertise.

Work left undone is overwhelming and daunting, and can feel like a large dark cloud hanging over you. What if you wrote a list showing the individual tasks that need to be done and the corresponding time each one takes? Lists can make it easier to get started, as it breaks down the workload – and getting started is often harder than completing the actual work. Using some positive aggression, or getting fired up, can provide a great sprint start that may carry you all the way to the finish line.

I feel that I've given my all.

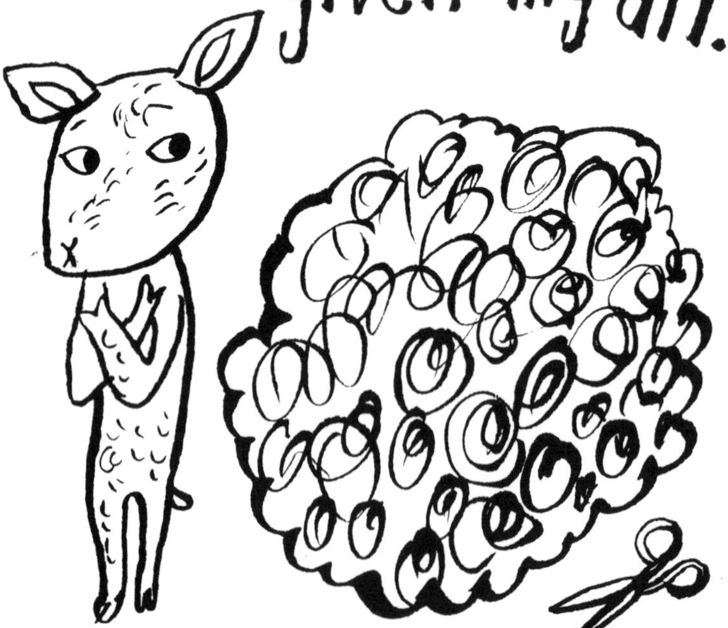

Even loyalty can sometimes be taken too far. Some people give themselves up to work all too completely. If you tend to be flexible, the boundaries between work and free time can easily become blurred. Being passionate about your work is great, but keep an eye out for signs of stress. How about stopping to look at what you have already accomplished, being happy with what you have done, pausing and regaining strength for the next task?

Everyone experiences setbacks in their daily lives, and no matter how hard you try to predict and prevent them, there will always be more. Working life is no different. Pay attention to your reactions and observe whether you are constantly living in a state of stress where your body and mind cannot recover from these small interuptions. There are many things that you can change, but there are also situations where all you can do is lift your paws up and let the fallen ice cream melt. Even then, take a deep breath, wipe off the stains, buy a new ice cream and take better care of it than the first one.

Employee
under
mainte-
nance

Every job is stressful in its own way, and an office worker needs recovery time just like an athlete. Taking a break will actually help with our efficiency in the long run. When we are tired, we can easily make mistakes and we will struggle to be truly present at work. Breaks are not a luxury or a chance to be idle, but rather about fulfilling an essential need. Well-equipped workplaces have spaces where you can sometimes relax, simply by stepping outside for a short time or even by taking a little nap.

I want to stay here until the working day is over.

Tired? Ask yourself what is causing the fatigue, and try to really examine the issues that are burdening you. There is no need to be ashamed of exhaustion, and you have the right to bring it up with your manager, colleague or health care provider. Have you been able to take breaks and give yourself moments of calm? Some of us are more sensitive to our environment and social situations than others, and therefore need more peaceful space and time to recover.

Burnout is discussed a lot these days. Yet its alarm signals still seem difficult to recognize, let alone take seriously. There may be outdated notions that working right to our limits is something admirable, or that running out of steam is a sign of weakness. What if the more 'sensitive' – that is, those who have more open emotional skills – are simply better at recognizing warning signals and therefore able to avoid more serious fatigue? Employee exhaustion can also be indicative of a broader, collective problem in your work community's culture.

Co-workers have a special vantage point on each other's lives, but opening up about our experiences may still feel like burdening others. If your colleague seems anxious or sad, ask them how they are doing. Ask if they need something. It is not intrusive to offer to listen. The least we can do is to try to behave in a way that creates an open and genuinely caring atmosphere in the workplace.

Often, we just lack the courage. We think we are respecting another's privacy. We do not want to bother others. But if we are concerned about someone, it is genuine care to ask if everything is alright. It is courageous and responsible to try to intervene. Some people naturally speak up, others curl into themselves. Many quietly hope that someone would ask how they are doing. When we dare to check in on a colleague's well-being, we also normalize talking about difficult issues and improve the workplace culture overall.

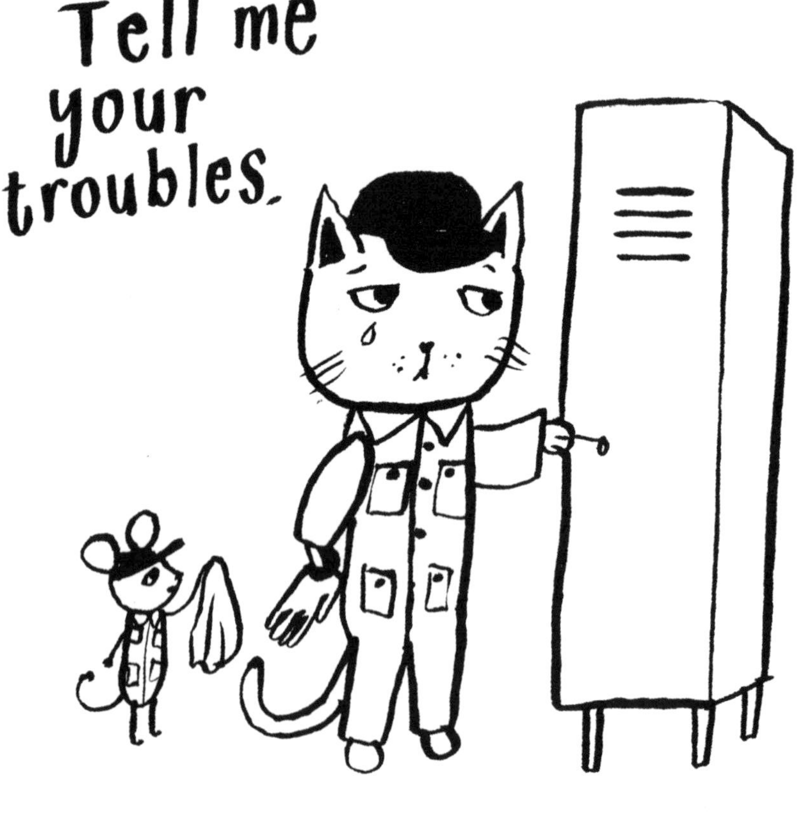
Tell me
your
troubles.

Sometimes the hardships of our personal life weigh on our shoulders at the workplace. We are not machines that can just turn off our feelings, it is perfectly okay to have feelings at work too. There are many aspects of working that are good for your mind; for example, many mourners find that the working day gives them something else to think about amid their crisis and in this they can find relief from their heavy, circling thoughts. Getting support from co-workers can play a huge role in grief or other challenging life situations.

Just
trust.

If you suffer from anxiety, work and the wider world can seem to be full of pitfalls and threats. A worrier thinks of things even outside of their job description and focuses on drawbacks rather than advantages. There are some things that are simply beyond our control and which require us to have confidence in the ability of others. Trust your abilities and your work community's capabilities, rather than always looking for weaknesses.

No matter what,
we are always here
for you.

One employee's personal crisis can affect the entire work community. A co-worker who is going through rough times is comforted by the knowledge that support is available and that they do not need to cover up the situation. There is no need to carry a secret inside while acting cool outwardly. Having a group of trusted co-workers – or even a couple of people who you can confide in if need be – can be a relief. A team to help you overcome difficulties. Facing challenges together strengthens the emotional bonds between co-workers and ties the team tighter together.

Nobody is defined by a single label. We all have our own particular mental health needs, which fluctuate throughout our lives. It is good to remember that everyone is unique and valuable exactly as they are. Work communities do not always know how to address mental health problems, so it is important to incorporate these topics into the workplace discussion culture. Are you someone who sees and accepts their co-workers just the way they are?

It's ok to feel blue.

Is struggling mentally a lesser reason to take leave than being physically ill? The threshold for talking to an employer about mental well-being should be low, and in a flexible, modern work culture, we should be able to take a couple of days off from work for mental health reasons without a medical certificate. The employer could offer the option of remote work or permission to stay away from stressful situations. An exhausted employee should be able to say, 'Now I need a day or two to nurture myself.' Taking the time for self-care and returning when they can work again, without guilt or shame.

One indicator of a well-functioning work community is how mental health issues are addressed. A colleague who has been absent due to mental health reasons may feel unnecessary guilt, so it is important that co-workers provide support and show care when that person returns from sick leave. Care and empathy can be shown in many ways, such as asking about their well-being and taking time to genuinely listen. Talking about mental health issues should be normalized at work.

Good communication is a sign of a healthy workplace atmosphere. In an open and tolerant environment, it is easier to open up and share, even those thoughts and feelings that are not fully formed yet. When sharing, it is important to be able to truly listen to what the other person is saying and not just focus on pushing your own agenda. Both sides of the conversation are responsible for a successful interaction, and a constructive exchange of ideas is the result of a unique combination of two minds.

There are too many
question marks in the air.

When we do not know how to relate to others, when personalities and communication styles are starkly opposed, and when conflicts are tiptoed around, the air suddenly becomes thick with question marks. However, the ultimate goal is to find a solution together, which requires listening to others, understanding and empathy. After all, the best solution may be found in the thoughts that have not yet been spoken out loud. Ask what the other person thinks, even if you do not understand their thoughts at first the resulting discussion could reveal the perfect solution.

Disputes and disagreements occur in every relationship and within every community. When stalemates keep recurring, one of four roles are easily formed: the first is provocateur, the second is anger, the third is mediator and the fourth is the silent sufferer. Identify what role you naturally tend towards to better understand any unhelpful behaviours that may be getting in the way of a resolution. If the disputes keep repeating themselves, consider whether there is something deeper behind them. Are you actually arguing about something that is below the surface? Try to calm things down so that you can discuss the root causes and avoid overreactions.

Workplace tensions easily lead into bad habits. Without early intervention, passive-aggressive behaviour can become part of the culture in a workplace. Avoiding the situation or staying silent simply cause the issues to build up. Confronting the situation or speaking out may seem daunting, but clearing the air will be such a relief. Tensions will always cause stress, but open discussion helps towards a happier workplace.

It is easy to turn a blind eye to bullying at the workplace. In an old-fashioned work culture, interfering with one another's relationships may be perceived as inappropriate or uncomfortable, but ignoring the situation simply enables the bullying to continue. Some forms of bullying can be hard to spot. Are you aware of what is happening around you? Does this behaviour fit with your values? Do you step in when you see bullying?

we took a chance
and look at us now!

Assumption and bias cause some of the biggest pitfalls in communication. Often, we are deeply rooted in our positions and do not know how to raise concerns face to face. Tensions arise, and the more time we let pass, the harder the tension is to unpack. Do not be afraid to confront these issues. Create a safe atmosphere for discussion by learning to listen to opposing opinions as well as how to explain your own point of view calmly. Working together to build a solution is a heroic deed.

We create
balance
together.

connection

Workplaces are filled with various relationships, some distant, some close. Some people find common ground immediately, while others feel like they are not even speaking the same language. Willingness to listen and the ability to present ideas clearly and amicably helps to form strong connections. However, these relationships can break down if you focus on pushing your own point of view and neglect to hear what other people are saying. Every encounter is a new opportunity to build a stronger connection.

I'm full of untold stories.

Everyone creates their own story. As we approach retirement, it is natural to reflect on our career as well as our lives so far. Too often though, these stories and life lessons are not heard by others. Older employees have a wealth of experience from which younger colleagues could gain a great deal. There is a huge benefit in having people of different ages in the workplace or a circle of friends, and it is a privilege to have conversations with people who are not of your own age. The wisdom of older and more experienced people is not tapped into enough. Have multigenerational discussions regularly; it is fun and valuable for everyone.

It is important for all of us to feel that we are being heard and that we can make a difference. Those who have been struggling with a heavy load for a long time can easily give up and stop trying in the face of prolonged adversity. If the culture at your workplace is uncommunicative, it causes stagnation that is reflective of wider problems. This state of paralysis can spread and become the general mood. It is vital to break the cycle of negative thinking, even with small actions, to create hope and change.

Do you find yourself wondering if this is all there is? Is it perhaps time for new challenges? Would you be able to use your talent for something better? Many people mull big career decisions over and over. They are torn between commitment and their desire for change. Consider whether changing jobs is the right solution, or if the focus of your current job could be redefined. On the other hand, if you have been dissatisfied for a long time, is the job really worth it if other areas of life are suffering because of it? Work is important, but it is even more important to have a meaningful life that feels right for you.

Laying off an employee must always be handled with sensitivity and an open dialogue, as it is a delicate and very personal experience. It is never just about numbers. Maintain responsibility and professionalism by communicating the reasons for dismissal as clearly as possible. In addition, the departing employee must be allowed to feel heard, as they will no doubt be processing feelings of blame and injustice, as well as several other negative thoughts. The right words are a great help in creating a more positive experience for all involved.

Working life has changed. Nowadays, it is rare to have a linear, uninterrupted career – instead, we move between jobs, studying and various life events. During long careers, we can end up in situations where we feel we have already reached our full potential. It is important to accept change as a natural development. It should be encouraged. Businesses often want to keep their employees, so it may be possible to change jobs within the same company or community and still find variety and motivation.

Changing jobs provides a good opportunity for self-reflection. Few people stop to consider what work has taught them. It is a good idea to regularly pause and consider whether you are carrying unnecessary burdens. What can you leave behind? What should you take with you? You can reevaluate your working habits and think about how you want to act in your workplace going forward. You can set goals for your future and think about what is required of you to make them happen. What about the things you are leaving behind – can you feel gratitude towards those experiences? If you are holding on to difficult emotions, you may not be able to understand what you learned until later.

Each job has different values and goals. Few people are motivated by results and numbers alone, and the real meaning of work consists of intangible rewards, those that make us feel that we are doing something meaningful in this world. Discussions should be had to reflect on the values of the workplace. We walk together as a diverse but unified group and when values are shared, it is easier to make great things happen.

After
work

Everyone has situations where work follows us home, but if you find this is more the rule than the exception, something needs to be done. In your spare time, your friends, family or partner deserve your full attention, but you also deserve to relax and recover. Are the causes of the problem in the workplace? Is your workload excessive? Do you have space to decompress? What about other aspects of life? The transition from work to home is worth paying attention to. What can you do to help yourself enjoy your free time and relax? There are many things you could try in order to wind down after you leave the office: breathing exercises, commuting by foot, going to a coffee shop or enjoying an art exhibition before going home.

Into your arms.

The thought of being close to and cared for by a loved one can get you through the stress of the rush hour commute. This may be a partner, child, parent, friend or housemate. Even a small message from someone important supports the worker returning home; when we are tired and facing a long commute, it reminds us there is something else that matters and can help us cope in the moment. Whether you are returning home to family or to your own space, life is rich and full of meaning through the connections we have.

Greeting a loved one after a day at work is about returning to our mental home. How wonderful it is to see one another! Coming home is, at its best, restorative and affirming, a moment filled with love and care. It is important to be present in those situations, even if you were only apart for the working day. If you have a hard time disengaging with work, try to find something that helps you leave the day behind and be more present when you see your loved ones. The daily routine is waiting for you at home, but before you do your housework and cooking, take a moment to be with your partner. Both of you need to have space to just be. It is wonderful to be able to share your everyday life, share your feelings and listen to someone else.

After work

Sometimes people have different needs concerning their free time. One might have waited the whole day to see the other, while the other was looking forward to a moment alone with their thoughts after work. It is okay if after a hard day you want to browse social media for a while or decompress by reading the newspaper. However, it can be hurtful if you have made plans together and your attention is somewhere else. You should discuss expectations with your partner and decide when you will be present together and when is a good time for certain distractions such as social media. Being together requires communication and emotional sensitivity. If you voice your hopes, it leaves less room for misunderstanding.

Ideally, when you are at work, your thoughts are on work and the big questions in life move to the back of your mind. After work, however, life worries and stresses may come to the forefront again. It can be difficult to face the worries you had pushed aside for the day and to confront your fears and those big questions. However, these weighty matters will not go away by themselves – addressing them is important for your peace of mind. Fortunately, you do not have to do it alone. If you cannot talk to your nearest and dearest, professional help is available. Many try to escape by constantly being busy and always in a hurry, or seek distractions through hobbies or partying, only to realize that at some point they still must face whatever is bothering them. Anything can be dealt with if you first address the root issue.

What if you are finding it difficult to have a frank conversation with yourself? Many try to silence themselves, to reject their thoughts and sweep them under the rug. The mind will remind us of issues we try to keep at arm's length. Everyone deals with difficulties differently. Angry and irritable behaviour often conceals something else, such as fear, insecurity or other deeper feelings, and it is easy to hide behind the rage. It seems like the anger is giving you power, but it actually prevents you from facing reality. It is hard for us to be kind in response to a bad temper. It takes emotional skill and composure to see through the irritable behaviour and ask, 'Hey, what's wrong?' But these emotional skills can always be learned. You can also pose the same question to yourself when you are being grumpy: 'What is the matter, would you like to talk about it?'

When you think about a loved one, it makes you feel good. Why leave it at that? Why not take action? How exciting it would be to get a real letter again! Not only does it make the recipient happy, but it is also a beneficial activity for you, the letter writer. It is an aesthetic experience to go to a stationery shop to choose the perfect card or writing paper. Try writing a letter and enjoy your choice of pen and the colour and feeling of the paper. Writing a letter requires mindful presence, and your handwriting also contains a lot of emotion. Letters are thoughtful gestures and make life more exciting.

Let's make this ride
as smooth as possible.

Juggling work and kids is quite the rollercoaster. We switch from work to home life with the boss' words still ringing in our ears while children are already screaming for their own needs. You cannot escape the fast pace, but you do not have to strive for the perfect ride; somewhat smooth is enough. Sometimes you can look at your life from a distance and see the beauty of the rollercoaster. At times, there is that awful feeling at the bottom of your stomach, but the rises and falls are not that big of a deal if you remain confident that you can stay on board.

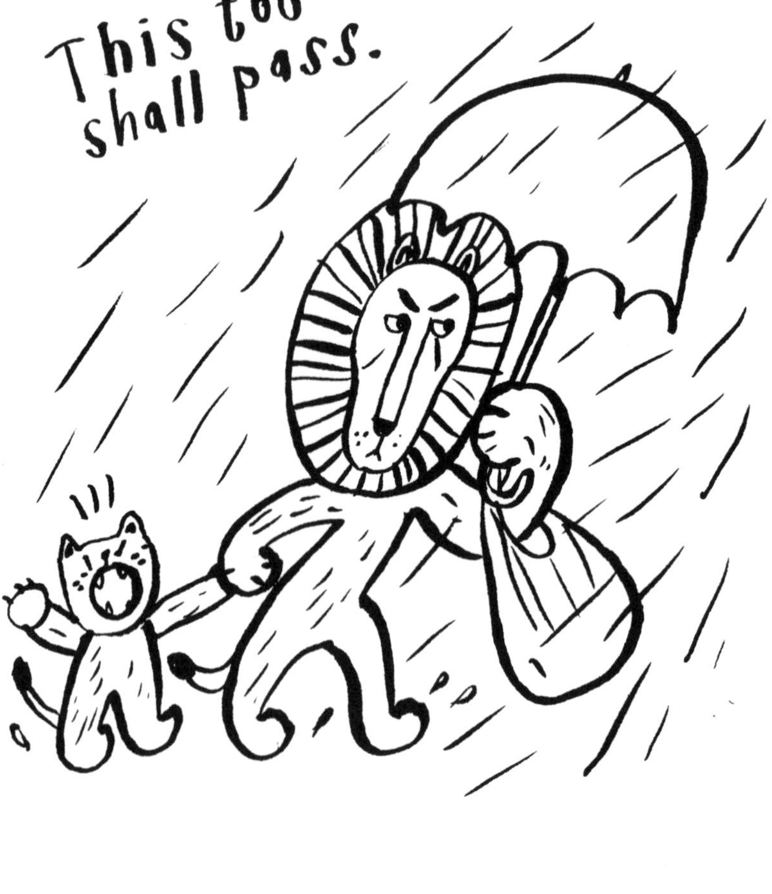
This too shall pass.

Every parent faces situations where their patience is put to the test and life seems to consist only of busy schedules and all kinds of demands. Your child is tired, you are tired and you both just want to get home. An adult can help soothe a child by calming themself first. A child cannot be expected to have the peace of mind gained by life experience, but an adult knows that no matter the frustrations of the moment everything will be alright.

Upgrade your after work.

After work, it feels nice to talk casually about work matters in good company, maybe with a good drink. However, it is easy to have a few too many beers or glasses of wine. Bear in mind that alcohol prevents recovery, affects sleep quality, and causes fatigue the following day. Having some social time is a healthy activity, but you can always choose a non-alcoholic option if you are going for a drink. Alternatively, exercise is a great way to balance the load on your mind and body, and you can still have a chat on the jogging path. Culture is also a great remedy for mental health, and through hobbies you can make new connections with likeminded people. Use your imagination and get creative – how can you relax and at the same time do something that is good for you?

In today's world, most office jobs are rarely physical. We exercise our minds, generally while sitting still. After work, you can find that rebalance in a different environment to help keep fresh and energized. Many of us have an inherent need to move, and we can think of our bodies as something that needs physical challenges. Sports, such as weightlifting, are not only about taking care of the body, but also engaging different levels of the mind. If our work is very abstract, it can be difficult to see progress sometimes. Something concrete, like exercise, can bring a necessary counterbalance and new sense of capability.

After work

Everyone can set goals and rewards for themselves, and there is nothing wrong with that. But if you reward yourself all the time, the value diminishes. Shopping can become a problem if you let the habit spiral and eventually you may find yourself in financial distress. Happiness cannot be forced through accumulating external possessions. It is worth noticing the difference between a short-term feeling of happiness and all-encompassing, longer lasting happiness. Think of other ways that you can reward yourself. Perhaps starting a savings fund and contributing towards greater financial stability could bring more profound happiness instead?

Most people have a sense of what is good for them and what is not. But it is challenging to put theory into practice, and old habits die hard when your sense and sensibility are at odds. For example, comfort food tastes good even though we know that too much is bad for us. We can be good at giving advice and guidance to others, and at the same time, be a little lost ourselves. Listen to the advice you would give to others and consider honestly if it applies to you as well. Healthy habits support mental health so build these into your daily routine in a way that is easy for you to sustain.

Be kind to yourself.

Giving in to a treat or a moment of laziness every now and then is not a crime. Our habits do not always need to be perfect, what matters is the bigger picture. In practice, we are never as perfect as we would like to be; it is human nature to have some contradictions between our values and our actions. Be gentle to yourself, but also notice if the bad habits start bothering you and your conscience.

None of us are made of steel. How we deal with setbacks and crises, tells us about our ability to react to change. We all respond in our own way to adversity in life, this is called resilience. Some of this is hereditary or learned during our early years, but we also build this strength through our life experiences. Whatever our current level of resilience is, we can always improve. Everyone's ability to problem solve, be flexible and have a hopeful view in life can be learned and strengthened.

When
we
face it
together,
we will
succeed.

By following your internal voice and daring to face your fears and uncertainties, you can find new strengths and personal growth. Have a conversation with your inner self. You can say to yourself, 'I have done my best, and that is enough for today. I dared to face my fears and found that they were related to my old experiences of failure. It is best to rest now and I will continue tomorrow.'

Evening

A happy life is a paradox; no one's life is happiness all of the time. If you read a biography of someone who is considered positive, you will notice that there is always something challenging, too; a small setback in their story. Happiness is all about seeing the bigger picture and emphasizing the positive aspects. No feeling lasts forever – that is part of the beauty! It is about surfing on the forever-changing waves of emotion. Even on a rickety boat, you can still get where you need to. A skilful sailor is an optimistic one.

If work does not offer the opportunity to live according to your personal philosophy, you can get involved with something fulfilling in your free time, maybe even together with a friend or partner. For example, many people are concerned about environmental and climate issues. Doing something purposeful and following your values gives life more meaning. By acting on what you love, it will help you recover from work and improve your own sense of well-being.

Evening

You being present is an affirmation to me.

Close, loving bonds make you stronger and physical touch helps to calm us, making us feel that anything is possible. Being able to take some time to rest with your loved one is reassuring after a day of work. In such moments you need no special setup, no special skills. Remember to take time for being close to your partner, as it strengthens your relationship and your mind. Give the other person time to think their own thoughts and, if need be, you can ask gently, 'What are you thinking about?'

Rise above
the noise.

Here is a typical weekday situation: dinner is not ready yet and everyone is frustrated, tired and hungry. Children scream while adults bounce sarcastic comments between each other. Sometimes it takes great skill to pause, count to twenty and stop the situation – which in itself is a perfectly normal everyday scene – from escalating and turning into a quarrel. Better control requires consciously calming down, taking a deep breath, and rising above the situation until you are able to continue running your everyday life again. Once you have food in your stomach and your mind has calmed, life will return to an even keel.

Some of us might put all our energy into work, yet our home looks like a rubbish dump. This chaos at home can represent our mental landscape. Free time is so often filled with taking care of things other than yourself. There may be life crises going on in your circle of friends; maybe your loved one needs a lot of support. When we struggle to set boundaries, we can find that we give everything at work and any resources we have left go to help and support others. Everyone has limited time and capacity, so you must pay attention to your own needs and prioritize them too. You should not feel bad about saying 'no' to people from time to time. It is important to take care of yourself so that you will be a better help to others as well.

Our space
has room
for both of us.

After a day of work, it is important to find time to wind down in the evening. Everyone needs their own space for a moment. You do not have to give up your hobbies and interests, you can coordinate them alongside those you live with. Giving and taking space is a skill and for many couples it is challenging to simply be in the same space without actually doing anything special. It is possible to be alone together. You can just be, side by side or even in different rooms, and an invisible emotional thread connects you. Living together is about balancing needs and respecting one another's interests.

Evening

planting
the seeds
of hope.

It is a wonderful mission for a parent to teach emotional skills and mental self-care to their child. A parent may, for example, have a dilemma in their working life or fall ill. Demonstrating a positive outlook on life during these times provides an important example for a child. There is always hope, no matter how dark things may seem, and you can always find potential and opportunity in the little things. If the atmosphere at home is one of despair or negativity, your children can easily adopt this attitude toward the world. If you are in a difficult situation, work together with your family to create solutions that will have a positive impact on the mood in the home and increase your confidence in your ability to cope. There are some things you cannot change, but there are also always those that you can. For a positive outlook, it is important to focus on what you can change.

Loneliness is a real but often invisible problem, and there are many lonely working adults. We often relocate for work or studies, and it might be difficult to establish new relationships, which can lead to unintentional isolation. The outside world does not always offer us things that feel meaningful, so it seems easier to, for example, stay in the world of games and social media. Reality is then seemingly more manageable, smaller, and feels like your own. This may bring momentary relief but is detrimental in the long-term. Once you have curled up in your own little bubble, it can be hard to find a way out, with no incentive to break the cycle. We all have a responsibility to look out for our colleagues. If you think someone is lonely and only living through their work, could you subtly ask if they would like to do something after work?

Our words can damage or heal. You choose.

Taking our feelings out on others is often a sign of a deeper issue. Those who are dissatisfied with work and life can sometimes behave well in the workplace during the working day, but the beast gets out on social media in the evening. If you lack the means to deal with your feelings, it is all too easy to be hurtful and spread your bad mood through online platforms. Often it is difficult to face things head-on, and the Internet offers a shelter from which to shoot unkind comments at others. Those comments are rooted in our own uncertainty and dissatisfaction. When you recognize a situation that triggers an emotional response, you can pause for a moment. The more emotional you are feeling, the better it is to think your words through before you hit enter. What kinds of things do you want to fill the world with? Are they constructive or destructive?

Good to hear from you!

Friendships do not have to be left behind in life; they can always be maintained. Even if a friend is far away, it is good to hear their voice and maybe even see their face through video calls. You can compare life experiences with a friend and share support. A friend has a precious understanding of you and can tell if all is not well and know the right words to say when you need encouragement. Still, a friend should not be used as a therapist; respect and enjoy the reciprocity and freedom of friendship instead. To have a friend as an adult is an incredible treasure in life!

I hope you know that you can talk to me about anything?

Are you someone who others can talk to and regard as trustworthy? It is an honour to be a listener, though it is rarely recognized as the special skill it is. We share the burden of life by listening and supporting each other. When you provide a favour, life will surely give you one back someday, but remember it is about giving freely rather than expecting anything in return.

Evening

Let's untangle this together.

Friendship, or any kind of relationship, can get tangled, and this can manifest as distance or irritation. Communication suffers and unkind comments hurt feelings. Each side shares responsibility; no one can fix a relationship alone. It is important to address the issue together and to recognize that there is a problem. To recover the relationship, it is often necessary to face the issue head on in order to move forward, and both of you need to take a proactive role. It is easy to be in a relationship when it is full of fun, but difficult situations require real work. Those who survive these bumps together take their relationship to a deeper level.

Carrying a secret often prevents us from being happy. It is a heavy burden to bear, taking up a great deal of energy. Secrets are often accompanied by shame and guilt, preventing us from living a full life. At some point though, you run out of strength and need to take the load off your shoulders. Only when you have relieved your burden do you realize how much it has weighed you down. People have different reasons to keep secrets: they may be afraid that people's attitudes toward them will change, that they will be rejected, or that they will not be cared for in the same way as before. Very often fears turn out to be unnecessary, and people are often more compassionate and loving than you might think.

Worries often prevent us from going to sleep. If you did not have time to think things through or the opportunity to talk to anyone during the day, your worries invade your mind at night and you cannot find calm. Even falling asleep becomes a source of stress. The wee hours are a time when we are at our most vulnerable and worries and pressures become magnified. At this point it can be a good idea to get out of bed for a while. You can also set up a nocturnal self-care box for yourself in advance. In the evening, make a playlist of soothing music or choose some night-time reading that will calm you down if you wake up. Keep a notebook and pen next to your bed so you can write down your thoughts and concerns. In the morning, you will see things in a different light.

Evening

There is an outdated habit of bragging about how little sleep you get at night and how long your days are. Almost nobody admires that anymore. Sleep and rest are essential. When we get enough rest, we can do almost anything – we evolve and we find clarity. When you are busy, resting decreases stress, helping you see things in a different light and allowing you to make better decisions. Healthy sleep and other types of regular rest are the best way to invest in yourself.

I know that
I'm cared for.

It is important to feel cared for. Everyone should get the chance to experience that. When you genuinely trust that you have caring and loving people around you, it provides a solid foundation for other aspects of your life. Having that sense of basic security allows you to be more independent and less reliant on relationships. Just knowing that you are cared for is like an invisible hug or a nurturing embrace.

Evening

Life is in many ways unpredictable. It is important to let things come and go. Daring to go with the flow and trusting that it will work out is a sign of a well-balanced life. Try to have an optimistic approach and to be curious and open to possibilities in life. When you do not plan too much or set too many boundaries, you can allow yourself to experience the unexpected good. Confidence in the future helps us navigate the waters of life.

Together through the hours.

We all have our ups and downs. When one of us is doing well, we can better support another. The next moment, these roles may reverse. This variation is part of the give and take in a relationship. Although we travel side by side in time and life, we all have our own stories and journeys to make. Everyday life does not have to be a struggle, it is a shared adventure. Let's support each other through the hours and days.

Evening

Working during
challenging times.

Across the stormy seas.

You only need two people to form a strong team. Together, it is easier to make life decisions and discuss threats or opportunities. You can get support from your spouse, a friend or someone close to you; it is important to remember that you do not have to cope alone in this world. In the storms of life, you learn about yourself and your relationships; it is an opportunity for discovery. Crises can teach you new skills, strengthen your relationships, and help you view yourself as a fighter who always makes it through.

Storm in a tea cup.

Life can throw all sorts of curveballs at us. There may not be a problem within a relationship, but external pressures make it hard to cope. For example, recession, unemployment, a financial crisis or illness can put all our resources to the test. If we find space for calm, it is easier to look at things with perspective. When the storms of life are tossing your boat around, it is hard to see things in the right proportions. Use energy-efficient thinking by considering what the essential issues are, and what are the ones that are not worth concentrating your efforts on right now?

Challenging times

I want to break all the mirrors in the world.

Life crises, such as burnout, divorce or the death of a loved one, can cause intense emotional distress. The feeling of helplessness and the disappointment in our limitations can feel paralyzing and may present itself as different forms of anger. In turn, the tense atmosphere can be difficult for people close to you to bear, which can further increase tension and lead to arguments. This is when the alarm bells should sound – what is the cause of all these symptoms? Seeking professional help may seem like a big step, but in the end, it is worth it.

Challenging times

Look at yourself with kindness and make peace with yourself. You do not deserve to feel terrible. It is possible to see yourself in the mirror, even a broken one, and think of ways to be a little less hard on yourself and to break the spiral of self-criticism. Perhaps work stress led to behaviour that you regret at home? Maybe you did not rest and recover enough and forgot how valuable you are? Are there areas in your daily life that you could improve to make yourself feel better? Could you add more opportunities for relaxation and recovery during your free time?

Challenging times

We are living in challenging times and crises such as the recent global health pandemic have led to social isolation for many. While isolation is a key means of protecting against the virus, it means that many people have been cut off from mainstream society for prolonged periods of time. COVID-19 affects people globally, yet we are all impacted differently. Crises such as this often exacerbate inequality and there are many people who are less protected than others. Let's not close our eyes to this inequality. Everyone deserves to be treated with dignity and respect. Behind every story there is a precious person.

Challenging times

Ground yourself with positive action.

In moments of crisis, feelings of uncertainty and insecurity increase. The mind is under greater stress and self-examination. It is important to remember that there are always things you can do to change your perspective. Small and everyday actions have a positive impact on our mental well-being and help us navigate through difficult times. A good routine helps us be mindfully present in the here and now.

Challenging times

In challenging times, loneliness may be exacerbated for those living alone, especially if we are prevented from socializing with others as we normally would. It is important to stay connected, even if that is in new and different ways such as virtual dinners or workouts. We all have a responsibility to look after one another, so think about your friends and loved ones and if they would appreciate an invite to a virtual catch up or event.

There is no excuse for selfish behaviour.

In an emergency or in times of need, we seek a sense of security and control. Taking action such as panic buying or hoarding may seem like a way to find reassurance. However, selfless acts and consideration for others are a much more effective route to peace of mind. We are all in this together.

Not every home is about board games, baking or outdoor activities. There are many homes where tension, fear and violence, or the threat of them, are present every day. Now more than ever we need to care for our neighbours and loved ones. If we hear furniture falling, chairs being thrown or angry yelling, we need to be alert to what is happening. Everyone has the right to feel safe at home. If you are concerned about a situation, seek professional advice or contact the police.

Challenging times

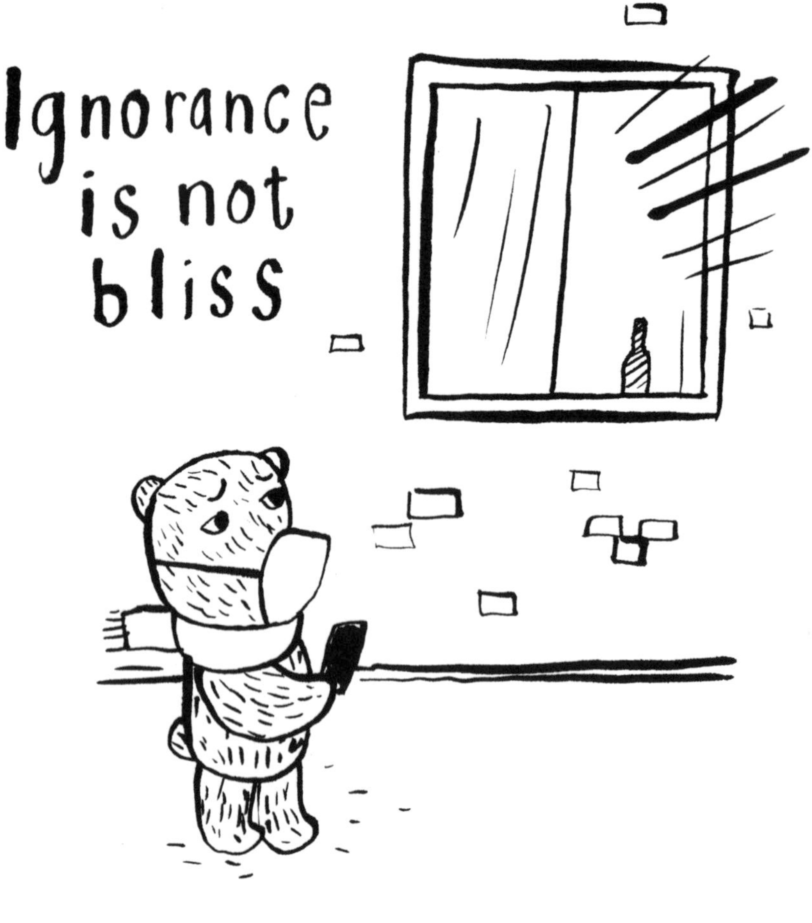
Ignorance
is not
bliss

If you, or someone you know, are experiencing abuse, visit the sites where you can find support from national online and telephone services. Contact the police, social services, a domestic abuse and violence shelter or other assistance organizations. In the case of an emergency, you should always call your local emergency number.

Challenging times

Despair and fear are fought through acts of care, reassurance and listening. Although we must be physically more distant from others at times, we can use creative measures to be emotionally closer. In periods of difficulty, we need each other more than ever.

Challenging times

In life, we will all experience difficult times. We can support one another by coming together to care for the most vulnerable and creating a climate of prosperity through wider compassion.

Even in difficult times, it is important to pay attention to the good in life. Take a moment for yourself every day and think about what you are grateful for right now. Gratitude can be shown through positive action and showing compassion to ourselves and to others.

Mental
health
made
visible.

CupOfTherapy™

CupOfTherapy is an internationally renowned concept addressing well-being and mental health issues through personal, easily approachable animal figures.

The CupOfTherapy world was created by Finnish psychotherapy professionals Antti Ervasti and Elina Rehmonen together with an awarded artist and illustrator Matti Pikkujämsä.

ANTTI ERVASTI (born 1975) is a psychotherapist specialising in family, couples and sexual therapy. He also gives lectures and addresses several sexuality related issues such as identity, relationships and violence in his workshops and lectures.

MATTI PIKKUJÄMSÄ (born 1976) is an award-winning artist and illustrator. He is known for his portraits and numerous children's books and press illustrations. In addition, he has designed textile and china patterns for clients including Muji, Kauniste, Lapuan kankurit and Marimekko.